MISS IDA

The Story of Ida Shumaker

Compiled

by

ANETTA C. MOW

BRETHREN PUBLISHING HOUSE
Elgin, Illinois

Ida Cora Shumaker

DEDICATED

to

all those who loved

MISS IDA

Contents

Illustrations

One of the most sacred privileges I have ever had was to care for Miss Ida during her final illness. For five weeks she was with the Doctors Cottrell and me in our home here at Bulsar where we could give her all possible attention.

In my days of training as a nurse and during the years that have followed I have had many patients, but never have I cared for one who co-operated so fully and who was so patient as Miss Ida. She never wished to cause extra work and she never wanted special attention. She made her doctors and nurse feel that she appreciated everything we did for her. Therefore I look back upon her illness with reverence and I feel a deep gratitude that I could serve as her nurse in those last days.

Not only in sickness but in health did Ida Shumaker show her concern for others. Those who worked closest to her appreciated her generous spirit the most. It can truly be said that those who were her friends loved her with increasing appreciation. It has always seemed especially significant to me that her co-workers who lived and worked with her day by day always testified that she never spared herself but gave freely and joyously of her spirit and energy, time and means to help everyone about her. Her loyalty and friendship held equally steady through times of persecution and criticism, and through times of prosperity and praise. They knew she loved them, whatever their condition might be, because she was moved with marvelous compassion.

When I heard that this account of her life was being prepared I was glad and I prayed that the ideals and qualities of her life might be so portrayed and the facts concerning her work might be so reported that her spirit should continue to live on in the hearts of all who read it. The author has spent many hours in assembling this information from records in our church publications, from letters and from the spoken word of friends. And now I commend this little volume to all those who knew Miss Ida and to many others, especially the young people of the church, who should be inspired by her life. Would that all who read these pages might know with her that

> *They who trust Him wholly*
> *Find Him wholly true.*

Verna M. Blickenstaff

Bulsar, India

Preface

Ida Shumaker's life was a life which inspired many people to a deeper love for missions in the sharing of Jesus Christ with the people of India; and so it was a definite joy to accept the assignment of writing her life's story. Many hours have been spent in reading through the volumes of the Missionary Visitor since 1910 and the articles and items of news in the Gospel Messengers which gave information concerning Miss Ida and her work. If such a task has been work, it has been a labor of love. Also letters have been written to her co-workers, friends and family, and many items of interest have been contributed.

The material in this small book has been gathered from church papers, from letters and from conversations with those who knew her intimately and from those who knew her but a short while. The author rejoices in the fact that she has been a long-time friend of Ida Shumaker and that for fourteen years we were "laborers together with Him" on the India field. And always it is with a deep sense of gratitude that I recall the first days of our acquaintance here in America when she in her gracious way put me at ease in strange surroundings. She had invited me to be her guest at luncheon on the train, and we were served strawberry shortcake. Who could ever forget such kindness of a missionary on furlough to a timid young girl who had never been in a dining car before!

This incident is mentioned here because it is so characteristic of Miss Ida. She was always doing the kind and generous thing for others.

It is believed that the church at large will feel thankful to all those who have given information.

Sister Ida's life was so filled with that spark of inspiration and glow of emanation that it has not been an easy task to capture this glory of her personality and put it into words. Her whole being throbbed with the desire to make Christ known and loved. She overflowed with enthusiasm for the sake of the kingdom of God. It can be said of her in the adapted words of this poem:

She lived in deeds, not years, in thoughts, not breaths;
In feelings, not in figures on a dial,
She counted time by heart throbs.

> *He most lives*
> *Who thinks most,*
> *Feels the noblest,*
> *Acts the best.*

From the biographies of lives wholly dedicated to Christ, every reader should receive inspiration and blessing. Within our church's missionary experience there are many life stories which should be written and widely read in order that we might know what these men and women of God have done for the sake of the church and for the kingdom. This story of Ida Shumaker's life has been written with the hope that all who read it will share the fellowship of her spirit.

Anetta C. Mow

Elgin, Illinois

MISS IDA

The Story of Ida Shumaker

SAVED TO SERVE

> Life is a mystery, a deep and relentless mystery,
>   Too deep for fathoming.
> Life is a gift, a rare and priceless gift,
>   Too rare for thoughtless living.

CHAPTER I

Saved to Serve

"Behold, what God hath wrought" is an exclamation that was often heard from the lips of Ida Shumaker. She was stating in her own way the same words of rejoicing which men like Job, Daniel and Paul had felt when they were conscious of the marvelous work of God. Ida Shumaker was keenly conscious of God's presence and his great power. So often did she break forth with this refrain that it may truly be said that it was one of her life's mottoes. She had many others and all found their origin in the deep fountain of her Christian experience and faith.

One day in the late summer, October 27, 1873, into the home of Alexander E. and Lydia Lint Shumaker, who lived in Meyersdale, Pennsylvania, a baby girl, their fourth child, came to live and bring happiness. They named her Ida Cora Shumaker. She had two brothers and three sisters: Anna, William, Margaret, Emeline and Frank.

Ida grew like other children and attended the public schools in Meyersdale, yet somehow there was something manifestly different about her. God had His hands on this child from her beginning, and manifested Himself to her even during her early years. She felt His presence when quite young; especially was this true when with a smaller sister she was miraculously saved from drowning. From then on she felt that God had saved her life for a purpose and that she belonged to Him.

At the early age of eleven years she taught a class in the primary department of the Sunday school. She not only taught but she helped wherever she could. At fourteen she made the public confession of her faith in God by baptism and united with the church. From that time on, in a more devoted way, she helped wherever needed.

Miss Ida was one of the first two to graduate from the Meyersdale schools. She was sixteen years old. She then began her teaching career, which lasted in America twenty-one consecutive years. Her summers were given over to further education, to lecture tours, to Sunday-school work, and to other interests. When Jacob Riis, the noted lecturer, met her and saw her work he said that now he had seen two people who knew how to handle children. Her county superintendent said she had no superior in primary work. She did have a unique way of handling youngsters. She loved them and they loved her.

During these years Miss Ida devoted much time to church and Sunday-school work. She had charge of the beginner and primary departments. She was the home department visitor on a route which covered ten miles and included twenty-nine members. She was called many times into homes where there was trouble, sorrow, sickness or death to read or pray for the people. She al-

14

ways went never thinking of herself and never seeming to get tired. She did much missionary work among the Sunday schools of Western Pennsylvania with Brother Ross Murphy, who was then the district secretary of Western Pennsylvania. For two summers she did home mission work in the Pittsburgh congregation.

A rich life of enlarged usefulness seemed to be taking shape for service in America, and then came the call to go to India. At the time of her baptism she had pledged her first allegiance to God, but now she found herself struggling to know God's will for her life even while she believed that she stood at the threshold of a life in which she could serve well. On one hand she thought that she could never be a missionary because she felt she was not in the least worthy. On the other hand she had to face the question of giving up the joy of having a home of her own and all that its companionship would have meant to her. For two years Miss Ida battled against the call and she had written a refusal to the General Mission Board. Then one night when she was sitting at home quietly having her devotions everything was suddenly changed. In a moment of clear revelation she saw her Lord and she knew what he would have her do. Also it was as if a small child beckoned her to come to India. Now she knew that God had spoken personally to her and that she was to go to India and work with the children of that great land. Her surrender was made and with it came peace and the calm assurance of God's blessing. She wrote another letter to the Mission Board saying she was ready to go to India.

From that day forward, Ida always felt that those days of testing with their final victory had been of inestimable worth to her, for they had given her the necessary courage to face all that her life and work should bring. She knew without a doubt that God wanted her in India; so she never doubted when difficulties came. Even when a doctor warned her that she could not live more than six months in the hot, unhealthy climate of India, she smiled and said, "My God will take care of that; if the Lord sends, He gives the power to go and do and say."

Her definition of a missionary was "God's man or God's woman in God's place doing God's work in God's will for God's glory."

In June 1910 at the great missionary conference held at Winona Lake, Indiana, Ida Shumaker was approved for service in India and Minerva Metzger for China. Elder D. L. Miller was the chairman and Steven Berkebile, who had recently returned from India, led the devotions. It was a day of high inspiration and dedication for Sister Ida. She returned home to make final preparations for sailing in the fall.

*To the Sunday schools of the Western District of Penn-
sylvania—loving greetings to all; grace and peace be
multiplied. Beloved in the Lord, your beautiful, soul-
inspiring message is mine. God alone knows what it
means to us to receive such messages of love, hope and
good cheer. Such messages are a source of great joy and
encouragement. They fill one with renewed zeal and de-
termination to push forward in the work of the Master.
Permit me at this time, and in this way, to thank you
most heartily for the same, and not alone for the message,
but also for your generous "gift for personal needs as the
Lord may direct." Words fail me when I try to tell you
how much I appreciate the message and the gift. The
dear Lord bless you abundantly and reward you accord-
ingly. Truly God has been good to us and has been
blessing us richly in all things! It therefore becomes us
to "sing praises unto our God, sing praises." May we never
grow weary in well doing, but may each year find us doing
still "more and better work for Jesus." What a joy to
know that you are not only ready but willing to make
the necessary sacrifice to support two, instead of one, on
the foreign field! God be praised! Your blessings shall
now be twofold. Surely the angels of heaven must sing
and rejoice. Let the good work go on! Continue to do
God the honor to trust him. See if he does not even in
this life prove that "he that soweth bountifully shall reap
also bountifully." Since I have so recently written you a
lengthy message I shall say no more at this time. Continue to pray most earnestly for the work and all the
workers. "Few can go; most can give; all can pray!"
So, brethren, pray for us.*

Yours in Christian love and service,

Ida C. Shumaker

January Missionary Visitor, 1913

I WAS NOT DISOBEDIENT

"I was not disobedient unto the heavenly vision."—St. Paul (Acts 26:19)

CHAPTER II

I Was Not Disobedient

On October 26, 1910, the day before her birthday, Ida sailed from New York on the Campania in company with the Jesse Emmert family. Many friends had come to see them off. It would be most difficult to describe the emotions which surged within her heart as the ship put out to sea and faces on the wharf grew dim. Ida experienced every one of them and her cup of joy overflowed when she went to her cabin and found waiting for her one hundred thirty-one messages filled with love, hope and good cheer from friends. As Ida tried to write her thanks to those who had remembered her, she could only say, "Remember the inasmuch."

After transshipping in Liverpool, England, the party went on to India, reaching Bombay on November 28. The next day Miss Ida came to Bulsar, which was to be her first home. As the train pulled into the station the party was met by missionaries and Indian Christians. Many bouquets and garlands of fragrant flowers were showered upon them. Then as they went on to the mission house they were surrounded by lines of schoolboys carrying torches and singing songs of welcome. Ida said that her heart was filled with joy and hope too full for utterance.

As with all new missionaries, Ida found the first months intensely interesting. During her first Christmas week she went with Eliza Miller for several days on a trip through the fisher villages of Bhat, Kakvadi and Onjal. She enjoyed all the experiences even when she had to wade mud and water two feet deep.

Miss Ida was filled with enthusiasm and she entered into her study of the Gujarati language with zest; so close was her application to her study that she completed the second year's course three months ahead of schedule time.

In fact, she was called upon to take charge of the girls' school at Bulsar after she had been in India but thirteen months. There were forty-one girls in the orphanage. Her work and her study fully occupied her time. Her days were crowded with duties and she was extremely happy directing the work of the girls in both the school and the dormitory. The girls were taught the arts of homemaking, such as sewing, mending, knitting, grinding, cooking, sweeping and washing.

The girls' school was like a large family and all the girls looked to Miss Ida as to an older sister. There was much sickness and there was death; there were weddings, many of them. New girls came and older girls left. Ida clearly remembered the time when sixteen new girls were brought into the Bulsar school all at once. This was when she herself had gone to the famous Mukti school to visit Pandita Ramabai and had returned with the group of new pupils.

She was always friendly with the girls and the teachers

and together they enjoyed many joyful occasions; however, she was a good disciplinarian and all knew that she expected honest endeavor from them. Once when several teachers persisted in coming to their work late, she said nothing for a while. But each day she observed the time when each teacher came to work and kept a record. At the end of the month when she handed out the pay envelopes, surprise and chagrin were written on the faces of those who had been coming late. All Miss Ida said was, "I'm paying you for the time you taught, not for the time you wasted." Nothing more was necessary, for the difficulty had been solved.

In India she soon discovered that the same satisfaction she had experienced in Sunday-school work in America was hers. Special emphasis was given to Sunday-school work. Throughout the whole of India there was an established practice of giving the All-India Sunday-school examinations in all Christian schools and our missionaries were glad to be a part of this great work. Ida gave herself enthusiastically to Sunday-school endeavor and each year gave more of her time to the Sunday schools at Bulsar and throughout the mission. It was always a constant source of inspiration to her that her friends in the Sunday schools of Western Pennsylvania were supporting her and her work.

It was a joy for her to prepare primary lessons for the Sunday-school quarterly. Her experience in America prepared her for this type of work on the field, and she was right in her element both when she taught her own classes and when she showed others how to teach. The

21

parents were made happy when they listened to their children sing songs, give Scripture portions and take part in the exercises of the Sunday school. Many of the songs they sang had been translated into their language by Miss Ida.

Although it always caused extra concern and work, Miss Ida was especially happy when the primary department outgrew its quarters. There were times when Kaliparaj (name for hill tribes) children of the Dubla and Dhodia castes came into her kindergarten class in such numbers that other rooms had to be found. Her heart went out to the Dubla caste children. She won their acquaintance and friendship and at one time there were one hundred sixty-nine in the class. There was also a mission band which she opened for the children who lived on and near the compound. The little folks enjoyed this class while their mothers were attending their women's meetings.

Miss Ida was grateful for the privilege of doing special teaching in the Bai Avabai high school of Bulsar each Saturday for one hour over a period of several years. More than two hundred intelligent boys from Hindu, Parsi, Mohammedan and Christian homes attended this school. She always felt that this was a great opportunity to teach and live the high ideals of Christ. She rejoiced when in later years a Brahman gentleman with his Ph.D. degree told her that her lectures had been a great inspiration to him in his youth.

Ida loved children. This was seen in many ways. Not a few grown-up men and women of today remember

22

those days when they were children and Miss Ida surprised them with a doll, a picture or some candy. She always had a surprise in store. One example of her methods was seen when she and some Christian children went into a new village. From a distance they had seen crowds of children and her hope ran high. But when they came into the village not a child could be seen or heard. The place was perfectly still. Miss Ida asked herself where those children could have gone so quickly and so suddenly. She looked up and down the road and not one was to be seen. Then she had an idea. She would stop long enough to place some bright-colored Sunday-school picture cards under some stones. Then she waited at a short distance and began to sing. As she looked up what did she see? There perched on the limbs of the trees like birds were many of the children watching every move she made. For a while they listened to the singing and then one by one they slid down. They secured the pretty cards. Soon from behind trees, huts and hedges came the rest of the children. They too wanted pictures. Soon the whole crowd came and such a service as they had! This was the beginning of further work in that village.

The missionary children also found in her a delightful friend. The majority of them remember many incidents in which Miss Ida gave them pleasant surprises, told them thrilling stories and inspired them to do their best. Many of the missionary children remember the times when she "took their picture" in her own special way. This usually happened at mission conference time when the children were together, having come from their various homes. Miss Ida would say, "Children, would you like your picture taken?" Everyone answered, "Yes," whether he knew what was about to happen or not. Then she instructed them to stand in line, and when all was in readiness she started at one end with a large tin box under her arm. Each one was asked to shut his eyes and hold out his hand. Quickly each hand was filled with candy — the hard, round kind — and the "picture was taken." With thanks and smiles and laughter the children would then scamper away to their play.

Whenever the opportunity presented itself, Miss Ida gave a gift of money to a missionary child as he left on furlough, saying, "Buy for yourself some little curio on the way home to America." Several of the mission family children, although now grown up, treasure their olive-wood New Testaments bought in Jerusalem or their picture or some piece of fancy work secured along the way.

For the missionary children who lived near or in the same bungalow with Aunt Ida, her room was a real mecca. They never felt that she was too busy to welcome them and entertain them. There was a glass cabinet in her room filled with beautiful little cups and saucers and other lovely dishes. For the children this cabinet was a treasure store and it was a red-letter day never to be forgotten whenever Aunt Ida gave a tea party and honored each child by asking her to drink from a beautiful cup.

Even her prized phonograph was graciously shared

24

with the children. She would give them careful instruction about its use and then turn the running of it over to them. They did not abuse her confidence in them.

Aunt Ida was a wonderful storyteller. Not only did the children feel shivers and thrills play up and down their spines when she told an exciting true story, but understanding adults were also intrigued by them. Who could forget her story about her own little finger bitten completely off by a hysterical schoolgirl, or the one about the sleepwalker who frightened folks in the dead of night, or that one about the half-witted gardener who attempted to hang himself from the rafters of the veranda? It made no difference whether her stories were taken from her own experiences or whether they were from the Bible; she made them glow and become alive.

Ida's first furlough came in 1917. She returned home by way of the Pacific. Annual Conference was held at Hershey, Pennsylvania, that spring and Miss Ida spoke to a large audience that hung on her words. This was to be true of all the groups that heard her during the length of her furlough period. Letters continually reached the General Mission Board from people asking that Ida Shumaker visit their churches. If she had come on furlough for a rest, rest could be had only through a change of program and not in a quiet retreat. No one knows in how many churches she spoke and how many homes she visited during the nineteen months she was in America, but the list would be a long one. She had stirred the imagination of many people and she had molded sentiment for India.

Hitherto Hath the Lord Helped Us

"Hitherto hath the Lord helped us."—The Prophet Samuel (1 Samuel 7: 12)

CHAPTER III

Hitherto Hath the Lord Helped Us

By the last day of 1918, Ida Shumaker was back in India and her home was at Jalalpor. This time the task given was to man the Jalalpor station and to start a school for Kaliparaj girls. The opening of this school was much opposed. And the opposition was increased and complicated by the entrance into the government high school of twenty Christian boys. When these twenty walked in, several hundred Hindu pupils walked out. Then followed strenuous days until this strike was settled. Miss Ida looked to the One who had called her to India. She kept her poise in Him even when prejudiced officials sent her an official notice to meet them in a distant village. Five villages were to meet and discuss the situation. She would be the only woman present. She dared to refuse the summons three times, but at last invited them to her bungalow. They came and the probable trouble was averted. The opposition was conquered. By the time the Christians were ready to dedicate the girls' school the number in Sunday school had grown to four hundred.

Then in 1920 Miss Ida was appointed to be children's missionary for the whole mission with her headquarters at Bulsar. She held institutes in all of the sixty-five schools then in the mission. And whenever she was at Bulsar she made efforts to find the Dubla children who had been in her class before she went on furlough; they were now scattered she knew not where in her four years' absence. After a three months' fruitless search, one day walking on the road and praying for her lost sheep she suddenly heard a voice and then two arms were thrown around her neck with the cry, "Oh, Missy Mama, why did you leave us these four years?" And she turned to find one of her lost children, still a small girl, but now a wife of four years with two little girls of her own. Through this little mother she found the rest and they all begged for another class in which they could again hear the Jesus story. Since she had no room in which to meet with them they met under a tree until a Christian family near by in Wanki offered their home as a meeting place. Some superstitious ones as they came into this home sprinkled water over their heads to protect themselves from defilement. But they came until the Sunday-school attendance soon reached four hundred and the last year before her next furlough the average Sunday attendance was five hundred fifty-five. Through this work the stronghold of caste was broken so that hearts were opened up for the reception of the gospel. Forty were baptized and a number of children also entered the boarding school.

When the 1919 Gujarat district meeting was held at Vyara, Ida Shumaker was one of the speakers. The message she gave concerning the progress of missions throughout the world was one that opened many eyes and broadened horizons for all who heard. Her vision was world wide and she longed that the Christians in India should realize the vast program of the kingdom of God.

The numerous duties which crowd themselves into the program of a missionary, especially when the attempt is made to shoulder the duties of others, usually take their toll. This happened to Sister Ida after a year and a half of heavy work, and she was ordered by the doctor to go to Landour for rest. For five months she was in the high mountains, where she regained her strength and had the rest she needed.

Bulsar again became Miss Ida's home in 1921 and she lived in her former "Retreat," a line of two rooms a hundred yards west of bungalow No. 1. Her time and energy went into work with the children at Bulsar, Wanki and Wankal. She felt that she should live for the children, for if India was to be won to Christ it would need to happen largely through the children. Christmas came to be an outstanding day for the whole community. Preparations were made far in advance of the date for the children to have part in the program. Not only did the children come but their parents also came. It was not unusual for eight hundred people to be present in the Christmas service. Doubtless the beggars and many others came for the gifts they were sure to get, but there were others, especially the Christian workers, who had so learned that it is more blessed to give than it is to receive that they had suggested that they put up a money box into which they could drop their mites each Sunday throughout the year in preparation for the gifts which they should give out at Christmastime. In one year their offerings had totaled thirty-eight rupees, eight annas (about $12.40).

During the four-month period when Sister Shumaker worked as children's missionary in the Gujarat area she traveled more than a thousand miles among the villages in the Dangs State, around Vyara and Jalalpor, and had a great many interesting experiences. This schedule of work always meant traveling in an oxcart or tonga over rough village roads and paths, sleeping in schoolrooms or out under temporary booths. She visited schools and Sunday schools and Christian groups at the main stations and also in the villages. Everywhere she went she gave interesting and profitable talks and showed the Christian teachers how to use better methods in their work. Under a *mandap* (booth) or under a spreading tree the people would assemble. Old and young, big and little, school children and their parents would meet together and enter into the exercises which Sister Shumaker directed with great skill and delight. To the Indian people it was an unusual sight in the village to see her persuade a hundred or more people to join in a game, when everyone forgot to be self-conscious and entered heartily into the fun.

When rich experiences came her way, Ida received them with overflowing appreciation. In 1924 she had the privilege of attending the World's Sunday School Convention in Scotland and the Keswick Convention in England. She considered this opportunity one of the most valuable blessings which ever came to her. She was profoundly grateful to friends who had made the trip from India to England possible. While in London she stayed with her very dear friend, Mrs. Jennie Weber, and together they planned how some gifts should be taken back to India for the village children. During her short stay, she interested a group of working young women in her work in India until they asked what they might do to help. This concern for others always was characteristic of Ida. She could not resist telling others of the work to which she had given her heart and enlisting their help and inviting them to deeper consecration.

Miss Ida's second furlough came in 1925-1926. Again she visited many churches throughout the brotherhood and attended the Annual Conference at Winona Lake, Indiana. Sister Shumaker directed the building of a typical hut on the conference grounds and she reproduced many scenes from India. These presentations made India seem more real to many people.

Miss Ida was invited to more places than she could visit. Nearly every place she went people were eager for her to come. However, once she had a strange experience when a local schoolteacher threatened to punish the pupils who should attend the church service. The older pupils went to hear Miss Ida talk about India and as a consequence the teacher demanded that each one write an article of several hundred words reporting what they had heard. Parents felt that some of the best papers ever written in the school were prepared at that time and that the teacher had doubtless learned more

31

about the land of India than he had ever known before.

Her contacts with young people in summer camps left lasting impressions with many. So thoroughly did she give herself on all occasions that the young people were irresistibly drawn to her. There was always enough humor and action to brighten every situation. Young people felt the pull of her personality and the attraction of her deep devotion. At Camp Harmony she met one young girl only twelve years of age who had been already writing to her for three years. This meeting proved to be the beginning of a most constructive friendship which lasted through the next twenty years until Miss Ida's death.

INDIAN SUNDAY SCHOOLS AND THE INDIAN CHILD

Our Sunday schools in India are as varied and as different as there are classes and conditions; but, everywhere you will find the child just as responsive, lovable and teachable as you will find anywhere (if not more so) if he has a chance. As Dr. Poole says, "The whitest part of the white harvest is the childhood of the world," and it is certainly true of our India. Therefore our Christian education must center about the child. We must place "the child in the midst" where Christ placed him. We must build our program around childhood and claim life at its beginning rather than try to reclaim it at the end. We must choose between tending lambs or hunting for stray sheep, for "the best and most natural way for a child to enter into his spiritual heritage is to grow into it gradually from the beginning. Only those ideals which have been built into the structure of character from childhood later become the dynamic and dependable factors in his life." And, as our own Dr. Kurtz said at Glasgow, "The supreme task of the race is the education of childhood. But the problem is to get the grown-ups to behave long enough for the task to be completed."

A great educator urged: "Let us live for the children." One of our greatest objects in all our Sunday-school work must be to find out how best we can give effect to that principle. It is the call of the child that summons every true worker to the task of bringing the child to its highest and truest development. This is our most important business.

If India is to be won for Christ it must be through the children. Herein lies our hope—our opportunity.

—Ida C. Shumaker, in January Missionary Visitor, 1925

WATCH GOD WORK WHILE YOU PRAY

"And Light and Strength and Faith
    Are opening everywhere!
God only waited for me till
    I prayed the larger prayer."—Cheney

CHAPTER IV

Watch God Work While You Pray

On her return to the India field late in 1926, during their first touring season she and the Wagoner family were out in the tent doing evangelistic work. They were in many villages and they went to some places where Christians had never been before. It was about this time that the mission decided that a self-supporting, self-governing and self-propagating church and Christian community should be established near the village of Khergam and Sister Ida was appointed to this task. A plot of ground about ten acres in extent was purchased.

The village of Khergam is about fifteen miles east of Bulsar, on the other side of the unbridged Auranga River, which is affected by the ocean tides. It is true that there was a large boat which was available at times but usually the river had to be forded. Often there were thrilling and rather frightening experiences for Miss Ida and her helpers as they crossed this big river. If they were late or had forgotten the rule of the tides, they found the high water already in and it usually meant either fording the river or waiting for hours until the tide went out. It was always somewhat terrifying whenever the cart and the team of oxen got beyond their depth and had to swim the rest of the way. Frequently everything in cases and baskets got soaked, even to the week's supply of bread. Once on such an occasion everything had been thoroughly drenched and Miss Ida's freshly laundered clothes were wet. After struggling through to the other side, she spread the laundry out on the bank of the river to dry. Even her postage stamps were soaked, and they too were laid out on the sand to dry. Women and children had watched them cross the river and feared they would drown. They crowded about Miss Ida and helped her to spread things out to dry, marveling all the while that she and her possessions were spared. They became her friends and from that time on they were happy to exchange greetings every time she passed along the road.

It was in January 1927 that Ida Shumaker, along with Brother Naranji V. Solanki and his wife, Benabai, and their family went to Khergam to take charge of the work. With them was a little girl always known to Miss Ida as the "nest egg." Elder Naranji and Benabai had been with Ida at Bulsar, Jalalpor and Wanki and they knew how to face problems together. The unfinished bamboo shed, the one little shoot of a tree, the unfenced compound covered with grass that even the goats would not eat, no well, no place to house the teachers—all this did not look very hopeful; nevertheless the three of them saw great possibilities in the small beginnings about them and they were undaunted.

Real work began. The promise of the "open door" was claimed and they moved ahead with the assurance

that God is love. They believed that by putting love
into action his work would succeed in spite of difficulties
and persecution. There was persecution born out of suspicion. Many of their neighbors were suspicious from
the beginning. Even some of the Christian teachers
throughout the district were fearful. When the announcement was made that a Sunday school and regular
services would be held each Sunday, they told those in
charge that such a thing could not be done. They feared
that even the children attending the day school in the
unfinished building would stop coming. They were sure
that such a bold announcement would prevent parents
from sending their girls to the boarding school. In an-
swer they were told that the work was to go forward and
Christ was to be lifted up before the people. The Lord
took care of the services, both the Sunday school and
the preaching hour, during that first year, and at the end
of the year sixty-five were enrolled in the Sunday
school and thirty-five girls were in the boarding school.
There had been strong opposition all along but the work
grew. There were baptisms and a communion service,
and then persecution flared up anew. The strongest opposition came when the first wedding was held, but in
spite of everything the Christian workers knew that the
hand of God was upon them.

At the first Christmastide, three thousand people gathered on the compound. The people were ready for a
celebration although they did not want it in the name of
Jesus. But Naranji believed in fearless and unapolo-
getic witness and in letting the people know from the

first where the Christians stood; so he gave the people a welcome in the name of Christ. To this the enemy took offense and an underground stirring up of suspicion began immediately. Then it broke out in virulent persecution. Many people were led astray until it looked to human eyes as if all the work of that section was doomed. But Miss Ida and her two faithful co-workers were not seeing with human eyes. Weeks were spent in traveling from village to village both day and night, trying to replace fear with hope in the scattered, terrified flock at each place in about nineteen villages.

The climax came on May 7, 1928. The whole Dhodia caste met in council. They called three Hindu *swamis* (ascetic religious leaders) to come and speak against the mission and Christ and thus incite the multitude gathered. The planned-for result was to go then in a mob, tear down the school building and return the girls to their respective villages.

While the mass meeting was in progress Miss Ida was in her room alone in prayer claiming the promise of the One who gave her this work and through whose name this persecution had come. And across the way in their own home were Elder Naranji and Benabai on their knees, too, in prayer. After some hours of agonizing intercessory prayer, Miss Ida felt the burden lifted and she was led to praise God for victory. Then she went to her co-workers and told them to arise and rejoice, for the victory had come. They wondered but joined her in praise. In a very short time a runner came from the mass meeting with the news that the *swamis* hired to curse had come with praise for the work of Christian missions. Like Balaam of old, they were under a restraint that kept them from doing what they were paid to do. To the instigators of the persecution this meeting was a failure, but to those who had spent hours in the presence of Him whose hand is not shortened the victory was the Lord's.

April 1, 1928, stands out as a day of great events, for on that day the Khergam church was organized. There were sixty charter members who gathered together in the little bamboo house. To add to the joy of the occasion, Brother Otho Winger, the chairman of the General Mission Board, was present and delivered the main address. A new church of Jesus Christ had been established and its members were determined to work for its growth in the entire Khergam area.

Ten years later there was in the Khergam church a membership of three hundred seventy. There were sixty-five Christian families living within a mile of the church. All the neighbors but a few had become Christian. Many continued faithful under continued severe persecution. Most of these families lived in their own homes. They paid for them through the help of their Christian Co-operative Society. The story of the upbuilding of the community cannot be told without a word about that Co-operative Society. It was organized in 1929 and six years later had a membership of one hundred eight and a capital of nine thousand rupees from Christians. The society was started with a government loan which was paid back in full and a loan from the mission which was paid back year by year. Over a period of several years the society was in fine condition, had a monthly income of about three hundred rupees and had only two or three delinquent members. A visit to the simple and inexpensive homes built through this aid, a walk around the numerous rice plots that helped to meet the owners' payments, and seeing the character-building pride of ownership and the keen interest in every spot made one realize that something very substantial had happened in the lives of the people there.

Near the girls' school, on another compound, a boys' boarding school was built. This boys' school building, brought to Khergam from fifteen miles away, was moved at the expense and by the voluntary labor of the Khergam church. Added to the more than forty in these two boarding schools there were day pupils coming from Christian families. And many Hindu children also came from the near-by village. The number staying in the boarding schools had of necessity been kept low because of the lack of funds. The vision from the beginning included having girls as well as boys in the mission schools, thus making the establishment of Christian homes possible. The Christian weddings and the founding of Christian homes during the following years have, therefore, been a great satisfaction.

But the story of the schools and the homes does not complete this picture. There is also the church in the heart of the community. Sunday-school children, grown-up school children, relatives and friends of Miss Ida's in America gave the money to begin the building of the

Khergam church. They gave the first half of the money
for the building. Then came the depression in America
and orders were given for all building to stop on the
India field. At this time only the foundations of the
church had been laid, and the doors and windows which
had been prepared had to stay in storage at Bulsar. Another season rolled around. Miss Ida was in the hospital
with a tired-out heart.

When the Khergam teachers gathered for their regular
monthly meeting with a burden on their hearts for Miss
Ida, they began to wonder if they could not do something about the unfinished church. One man offered to
sell his house and land and give two hundred fifty rupees
if they would proceed with the work on the church. And
so the work began. Miss Ida had from the first given un-
stintingly of her strength and yet she had not made any
of the people beggars. She had somehow built into them
her own sacrificial spirit. And that spirit now bore fruit.
Over seventy very poor members gave less than five cents
each. Naranji's father, who was the contractor and
builder, found great joy in giving his services completely
to the church. He would take no pay for the weeks and
months of work he put into the building, for he did his
work as unto the Lord. Other laborers gave their service
free also. Owners of carts used them freely to help in
the building. Teachers gave one month's wage out of
their meager money. This was over and above the tenth
they regularly gave. By counting labor value the people
of the Khergam church in one year had added four thousand five hundred rupees to the four thousand eight hun-

dred rupees which had come from America. Each morning during the erection of the building, Naranji, the pastor, had met with all the workmen for a period of prayer before beginning the day's work. On March 27, 1934, the church was ready for dedication and the building stood as a monument to the deep consecration of the Khergam Christians and the glowing faith of Miss Ida.

Throughout the years the Thanksgiving Day service at the Khergam church has come to be an outstanding event. Until the church building was built and all expenses were met, the service was held especially with the purpose of bringing in gifts for the church. Every member gave as he could. One promised some needed lumber, another promised days of labor, certain ones would furnish plaster, one man gave a tenth from his farm during the year, another brought a pumpkin, someone else gave a goat, and women and children gave as they were able of cotton, fruit, eggs, or rice. Visitors who came were deeply impressed and they marveled at the heavy burden which the members carried so willingly and gladly. Someone has said that church buildings can be built with sacrifice and prayer and much loving labor. Nor has the spirit of giving ceased since the church building has been erected.

These years had been filled with heavy duties and with the strain of concern and Sister Ida had felt the weight of it all; yet within her heart she sang songs of thanksgiving and she was happy in the little commonplace things of life. There was a deep-seated sense of humor in her soul which broke forth on most occasions.

All that is needed to prove this is to quote from one of her articles written from Khergam which appeared in the Missionary Visitor:

"You should pay me a visit in my real Indian house here in the jungle. Like Paul, it is a 'hired house' in which I live. It has mud walls and mud floors. You could enjoy many rare luxuries all free of charge. I have a spacious 'roof garden,' well lighted by moon and stars, the finest kind of electric lights. The birds and wind, nature's helpers, have made possible this garden on my roof. I also have a first-class orchestra—songsters of various kinds—with Mr. Toad leading the band, a cats' concert, in the interim, and many 'operatic spasms' when Mr. Snake appears. That makes me think of my 'conservatory' also. That is a story too long to tell, only this: A few feet from my house is a dense jungle. At present it is occupied by a pair of large cobras, which often appear, yet never stay long enough for us to give them a needed 'salaam.' One morning we were at prayer in my house when I heard a slight unusual noise. I opened my eyes just a wee bit and saw Mr. Snake come into the prayer meeting. I kept my eye on him to see which route he meant to take. He came in one door and kept close to the wall on the three sides (we were on the fourth side) and made his exit. No one else knew of this till the amen was spoken and they saw the 'tail end' of Mr. Snake departing. You see he came in right by me so I saw. Maybe that was a case of using the words, 'Watch and pray,' in another sense."

Early each morning the church bell, which was selected

and sent from England by Ida's very dear friend, Mrs. Weber, has called the Khergam community to prayer. The children have continued to come from the boarding school and all the families of the vicinity have come to this daily worship hour. Here they have united as a community in worship and Bible study. No one has ever entered the sanctuary without first removing his shoes. No one has thought of talking aloud. No absence has ever gone unnoticed. At the heart of all has always been the upheld Christ. "Seek ye first the kingdom of God," "And I, if I be lifted up will draw all men unto me," "Watch God work while you pray," and "See what God hath wrought" have always been the spurs which kept their faith undaunted.

An entire book could well be written about the growth of the church and the community at Khergam, about how the schools developed and how the surrounding villages were touched, about the growth of the Wankal community and the organization of the Bamanvel church, which was like a daughter of the Khergam church. Such a book would be also a picture of Ida Shumaker's labor of love for the eighteen years between 1927 and 1945. When impossible situations faced her and her Indian fellow workers they did not attempt to solve them in their own strength, but laid all before the Lord and trusted Him for guidance and strength. Elder Naranji V. Solanki and his wife, Benabai, worked with Miss Ida as constant and faithful companions. In the midst of great difficulties they rejoiced as they saw the directing hand of God. Wonderful services of thanksgiving and rejoicing were

44

held and the people came together for praise and the renewal of their vows. All of this made Miss Ida rejoice.

So rapidly did the years pass by that it seemed but a few years until it was time for her third furlough. As before, while she was in America most of her time was spent among the churches. Sister Ida was a popular speaker and many churches invited her to come. Planned tours took her through several church districts. Her messages were filled with inspiration and so personal was her contact that all who met her or heard her speak felt that she had inspired them to see new visions of opportunity. Here and there in many places are to be found those who say: "She has been a great inspiration to me," "Her letters are so full of joy that they are like a benediction," "She always made me feel that I had helped her," "She always said such nice things and appreciated every little thing." In one of the churches which had been very close to her and her work she was presented on Mothers' Day with a beautiful bouquet of red roses, and on the card were these words, "To a 'Mother' who gave up a home of her own to be a mother of the children of the world."

Once while on a tour where her strength had been heavily taxed she became ill, and in order to ward off pneumonia she was rushed to the local hospital. It was thoroughly characteristic of her that even on the short drive in the ambulance she should speak to the attendant nurse about India and encourage him to be a loyal Christian. All the doctors and nurses soon learned to know her and love her for her overflowing spirit.

WHAT HATH GOD WROUGHT

"What hath God wrought."—Numbers 23: 23

CHAPTER V

What Hath God Wrought

Again it was a day filled with abounding joy when she left New York on the S. S. Britannic on September 22, 1934, on her way back to her beloved India. This was her fourth term of service and again Khergam was her home. The members of the Khergam church rejoiced that she should occupy the rooms at the rear of the new church building. They had sent a special request to the Mission Board while Miss Ida was at home on furlough for her to return to them, and they were exceedingly happy that she should now dwell in their midst.

If details of her daily schedule during the next six years could be told they would make interesting reading. The work continued to grow and Miss Ida taught the Christians how to stand upon their own feet. There were times when persecution was strong against them. The Arya Samajist adherents felt it was their religious duty to ferret out those families who had become friends of the Christians. This caused constant agitation and distrust and it drove Miss Ida and the Christian leaders to their knees many times.

The oxcart and the small two-wheeled *damani* were in habitual use throughout the whole district as Elder

Naranji and Sister Ida made trips to visit the schools and the homes scattered all over the territory east of the river. Often during the hot, dry months she jogged along the roadside or across the open fields in clouds of dust. The shade of a tree looked inviting and frequently she enjoyed a short rest in company with a herd of cattle and all the attendant flies and insects. And then during the monsoon season more than once did the oxcart mire down in deep ruts and Miss Ida find herself wading out through the mud. In one of her letters she has given a picture of a monsoon trip which brought forth words of praise, not fear, from her lips.

"We were up at 2 o'clock in the morning for we had three schools to see in that section. We had already visited two and were headed for the third when suddenly the sky became inky black. We were yet on the bad country roads, away from any kind of protection whatever. We were driving in a clear open space with no house near and not a person in sight. I told the ox driver to head for the main road as we could not reach the third school. The oxen could not go very fast for the road was bad. Suddenly the wind burst upon us in all its fury. We were facing it. It seemed for a time we were to be blown away. Such a fierce hurricane it was! The driver looked at me in a helpless sort of way with a mute appeal in his eyes. I turned to him and said that God would care for us as He had promised before we started. The promise had been given to us as we had our devotions. He had assured us: "My presence shall go with thee." And now on the lonely, slippery road in the midst of the storm we just reminded God of this promise, claimed it, and went right on, carefully and slowly.

"I think I never saw a more beautiful sight in the heavens than I did then. The bright flashes of the zigzag lightning with such a dark background made a most fascinating display of electrical power. I saw the hand of God in it. The heavens declared the glory of God. This was followed by loud peals of thunder that seemed to shake the earth. Peal after peal echoed forth. Really, it seemed like great majestic music to my ears. I soon found I was singing This Is My Father's World.

"On, on we went, for we were yet far from home as well as a long distance from the main road. Now came the slashing, dashing, pouring rain! Soon the country road became as a wild river. There was water, water everywhere. In a very short time, the oxen were wading water knee-deep. We must put ourselves into the Father's hands and we trusted ourselves to the faithful, sure-footed oxen too. They could not see the deep holes in the ruts of the road, but they carefully felt their way along. 'There shall be showers of blessings' came popping into my head as I saw the brown, hard-baked, thirsty earth drinking in the freshness. And thus a note of praise and thanksgiving was sounded as on we went."

By actual experience she knew the truth of what she wrote for the Gospel Messenger when she said, "To build up a village Christian community challenges the best that is in one. It takes hard work. It also takes the labor of love and the patience of hope. We must go where the people are and live among them. We must begin where they are and then lead on gently but firmly and resolutely until the desired goal is reached, then move on to higher ground and keep growing. As we live among them as real lovers of their souls, we dare not attempt to change everything in a day, or to turn their little world upside down. We must share their joys and sorrows, taking lively interest in all the little details of their daily lives. It means implanting in every village the desire for its own improvement. We must build not only without, but within; then we shall be very conscious of the very presence of Jesus, for upon that foundation we must build."

During this period of service the Khergam church had grown until it believed it was time to take steps to organize a daughter church in the village of Bamanvel, about twelve miles away. In four villages, land had been deeded to the church for the local schools. In each village where there was a school the village people had put up the school buildings, had kept them in repair and had furnished everything except the Christian teacher's wages and his supplies. And the people were encouraged to give something toward the support of the teacher. As far as possible the people were led out on the principle of self-support and they were encouraged to be a self-supporting, indigenous church and Christian community. By their yearly thanksgiving offerings, their Sunday-school and church offerings, birthday offerings, special thank offerings and their tithes they were on the way toward self-support.

50

Although the work was difficult it was wonderful to see the growth and development of the village people when one considered the point from which they started and the conditions under which they lived.

To realize anew the pleasure Miss Ida got and gave on her visits to the village schools, one should reread her account of parents' day at Marla. The little village had outdone itself in making everything ready for a fine program. Some six hundred people were present. This was the day when Miss Ida was to hand out the prizes. As she arose from her high and narrow chair it rose with her. When she was finally set free, her dress was torn in several places. As she said, there was nothing else to do but smile and make the villagers feel at ease.

A number of great days stand out in the history of the Khergam church. There were the great thanksgiving services when everyone came, bringing an offering, the Christmas season, Passion Week, when the sacred baptismal rites were witnessed by the whole congregation, and there were the special services when someone of their number was called into the ministry or other office in the church. Visitors came from neighboring churches and missions. A deputation from the homeland, members from the Mission Board and friends almost always as they departed left with one of Sister Ida's verses upon their lips, "What hath God wrought!" When Miss Van Doren, educational secretary for the National Christian Council, studied the work at Khergam she said it was evident that a master mind was back of this whole project, for even the woodpile fitted into the picture.

Miss Ida was generous and unselfish to a fault. She found great satisfaction in helping others and she shared that which she had liberally. Her friends loved to give gifts to her and she in turn loved to give to her friends. Never did she keep back things for herself. The reason she accepted presents was that she might pass them on to others. It has often been said of her that she did things in double measure, for her liberality knew no bounds. And yet it is true that in her generous giving she always aimed to give in such manner as to help people to become more resourceful rather than to pamper them. One man expressed it exactly right when he said, "When I give I make beggars; when Miss Ida gives she makes givers."

By the end of 1940, Miss Ida had given thirty years of constant service to India and she returned to America. So unselfishly had she given of her strength that she was weary and none too well. All had wondered that she had not broken down but the Lord had sustained her marvelously. In fact, as she came back to the States, many thought she had returned to stay. As she took the train at Bulsar large numbers of her friends from Khergam and Bulsar came to bid her farewell. Many wreathes of flowers were placed about her neck and many tears were shed, for the people thought they would not see her face again. And missionary children pinned flowers in her hair and loved her for all the jolly times she had shared with them. On October 19, 1940, she and Eliza Miller left India's shores.

Her voyage homeward must have given her the rest

she needed, for shortly after she came home she received and accepted many invitations from churches to visit them. She was scheduled for tours among the districts and again her time and strength were given to her witness concerning India. It was not long until her friends knew that she was homesick for India. She could speak of little else than the tasks still waiting to be done in the Khergam area. She said she felt that there was still another chapter for her to write in India. Many of her friends prayed earnestly that the way might open for her to return, and her daily prayer was that the Lord's will should be done.

THE LORD HATH DONE GREAT THINGS FOR US

"The Lord hath done great things for us, whereof we are glad."—Psalm 126:3

CHAPTER VI

The Lord Hath Done Great Things for Us

And so it came about that after a four years' sojourn in the States, Ida was on her way back to the precious land of India. One congregation in Middle Pennsylvania helped her in a special way with funds for her return to attend the golden jubilee and spend a few years in service. Her trip back was a long and tedious one, for it was during the years of war. She and Lillian Grisso went by way of Lisbon and South Africa and reached India on the Western coast at Goa. They came to Bulsar just one week before the great jubilee celebration, commemorating the fifty years of the Church of the Brethren in India, began. Her prayers had been answered.

The motto of the golden jubilee was "The Lord hath done great things for us whereof we are glad." It was as if one of Miss Ida's chief verses had been selected for that great occasion. No one would be able to describe the depth of her joy during those days of corporate praise and thanksgiving. In spite of her years and regardless of the fact that she had recently ended a long voyage, she joined the long procession which marched four miles about the town of Bulsar. Walking in the midst of the women and the children she loved, she was very happy.

After the celebration had ended she went to her home at Khergam. The rooms at the rear of the church building were hers. She wrote to her friends that she had real fun in setting up housekeeping for the eighth time. So natural was it for her to enter into the work that she was immediately in the midst of it all. She was so busy that she found little time to write. She promised to write a letter for the church paper telling about her work at Khergam but it never came through. However, all who knew her knew that her work was a continuation of what she had done four years earlier. These were days when everyone was faced with increased hardships brought on by the war. Ida faced them bravely. Prices were high and provisions were scarce. In a letter to a friend she wrote: "We must make every minute of the day count for we get only a very small amount of kerosene each week to use in our lamp, and it is not enough. I do my reading and writing by daylight so that I can save a few drops of oil for the longer evenings during monsoon." Not for her own need was she concerned, but for the needs of the children in the school and for the people of the community and the villages. To the best of her ability, as she herself said, she rendered unto Christ her wholehearted consecration and service. And it was all done in Jesus' name and in the power of the Holy Spirit. Thus one year passed by.

Then came the cablegram saying that Miss Ida had passed away on February 16, 1946. She had been ill for several weeks with heart and kidney trouble but she had been too much occupied with her work to give her health much thought. Early in January she went to Bulsar for medical treatment, expecting to return to Khergam soon. Although she had the best possible medical and nursing care, since she was in the same home with the Doctors Cottrell and Nurse Verna Blickenstaff, her condition steadily grew worse.

She realized her condition and yet she was hopeful to the end. When Dr. Laura Cottrell told her one day that her heart would soon stop its beating and she would be at home with God, she said, "Yes, it will and all will be well." She had been anointed several weeks before and her faith was strong. Almost to the end she talked of work still to be done, yet she was content when God said she had done her part. She thought of her going as entering a new and more glorious life. On Saturday morning she passed quietly into rest.

At four o'clock on a Sunday morning the funeral service was held on the front veranda of this medical bungalow. Many Indian friends from Khergam and from the Bulsar community and the small group of missionaries came together and in the glory of a bright full moon heard the reading of Scripture and the words of commendation spoken for one who had been faithful to the call and commission of God.

D. J. Lichty, Naranji V. Solanki and T. B. Jerome had charge of the service. The message of First Corinthians fifteen was read and a short account of her life was given. Then Brother Solanki, who with his faithful wife had been her co-worker for many years, read from Romans 8: 28-39. He spoke of her untiring spirit and her great joy in giving the best she had to the One she loved best, and of the double portion of service she had always rendered. His tribute was sincere and all who heard him speak knew his words were true. This service was conducted in Gujarati. From the bungalow all went to the English cemetery, where Scripture was read and a prayer in English was offered by Brother Lichty. Then Miss Ida's body was laid to rest.

Three weeks after her death, when the annual conference met at Bulsar, the missionaries who could not be present at the funeral came together for a memorial service. The following resolution was prepared:

"RESOLVED: That the missionaries assembled in annual conference at Bulsar, India, hereby record their deep sense of loss in the death of Sister Ida C. Shumaker, which occurred February 16, 1946.

"Sister Shumaker came to India in 1910 and served continuously for a period of thirty years; then, after an absence of four years, she was privileged to return for the jubilee and another year of service. Her zeal and devotion to the cause, her sacrificing spirit and her unflagging energy were a continual inspiration to her coworkers and the church in India. She was widely known as an expert teacher of children, and was greatly loved by those whom she had taught throughout the years. 'Aunt Ida' was also a great favorite of the missionaries' children, for whom she always had a cheery word, an exciting story, and a bit of candy or cake.

"We praise the Lord for her inspiring service and her

zeal for the Master's cause, and pray that He may send forth others to carry on the great work which she laid down when she was called to her eternal home."

The Joint Council of the Church of the Brethren in India passed the following resolution:

"We are extremely sorry to take note of the sad demise of Miss Ida C. Shumaker on the 16th of February, 1946, at Bulsar.

"Considering her experience, her deep love and sympathy for the Indian Church, her unbounded zeal for her work, her loving and sympathetic attitude towards adults, children, males and females of all castes and creeds and especially her work and encouragement for the uplift of womenfolk, her death will be an irreparable loss to the Indian Church. Her love for the Indian Church is clearly revealed in this, that even after completing the period of thirty years of service, instead of getting retired she came back to India and served the Church for one year more, until the time of her death. Her memory will always remain fresh and green in our hearts. The Indian Church will always remain indebted to her for her unstinted work and services."

The church in America as well as in India had been blessed by her life. Friends everywhere felt a spirit of benediction upon them when they learned of her departure. In many churches throughout the brotherhood, even among groups that had not known her long, memorial services were held. In her own childhood church at Meyersdale, Pennsylvania, a tablet was erected to her memory.

The General Mission Board has endorsed most gladly the request which came from the Joint Council of the Church in India that in honor of Sister Shumaker a memorial school building shall be built at Khergam and memorial cottages shall be built in surrounding villages for village evangelists and pastors. As this call goes to the churches of the brotherhood, it is sent out with the prayer that many friends will respond and thus help to carry on the work which was so dear to Sister Ida's heart.

The chapter she desired to write in India proved to be the last chapter of a life wholly dedicated to Christ in behalf of India. Only eternity will reveal the contribution she made during the thirty-five years she gave of herself for the growth of the kingdom of God in India, and especially during the last year, which was wholly dedicated to the people she loved so dearly. She had stood watching God work and His presence had gone with her even unto the end.

Tributes From Fellow Workers in India

IN MEMORY OF SISTER IDA

J. M. Blough, Vyara, India

Who can estimate the value of Sister Ida Shumaker's last year of service? One year of guidance, one year of united prayer, one year of fellowship, one year of encouragement and teaching to trust the Lord fully—who can measure the value of such service? God does not count time as we do. Her enthusiasm and example of devotion and sacrifice have always been a great inspiration to others to live better lives and to work more diligently for the Lord.

It is befitting that she should pass her last days among her fellow workers in the land of her adoption and that her body should rest in its soil.

The missionaries assembled in their annual meeting held a memorial service on the fifth of March. In it many testimonies were given concerning her sterling qualities and Christian virtues. She came back to India because she believed firmly that her work was not finished here. She was eager to do still more for the spiritual growth of the Khergam church. She excelled in devotion to duty, stedfastness, self-sacrifice and liberality. She became poor to make others spiritually rich. She was very conscientious and could not be turned away from what she believed was right. She was devoted to her Lord and her Bible and led a life of prayer. She was most unselfish, always doing things for others and desiring nothing in return. She was an excellent correspondent and kept in close touch with many friends in America. She was an expert storyteller and teacher of children, and thousands will praise the Lord for the privilege of sitting in her classes both in day school and in Sunday school. She is gone but her spirit lives among us; her work is ended but her influence will live forever.

IN APPRECIATION OF SISTER IDA C. SHUMAKER

Elder Naranji V. Solanki

On behalf of the Khergam church, India

When Sister Shumaker returned from furlough in 1926, she was appointed to Khergam to open a village boarding school for girls. At this time there was only a compound without a fence, a small tree and a small bamboo house which was not yet finished, with no houses at all for teachers or for herself. But she and the workers were not discouraged; they began with a victorious spirit. She rented a small house on the edge of town which was without conveniences. On the twentieth of January, 1927, when the first girl came into the boarding school, Miss Shumaker was very happy.

In the face of opposition she, with the power of love, built up the boarding school on a good foundation and made it strong.

To strengthen the school and the Khergam church after 1927 she traveled through the villages, made many friends, increased the number of village schools to twenty-one and made them an evangelistic agency. She began the evangelistic work with such zeal that in April of 1928 the Khergam church was organized.

Miss Shumaker by spending herself and her means night and day put the Khergam church on its feet. In this she was willing to spend even her last cent; in order to establish the Khergam and Bamanvel churches she labored without rest and finally gave even her life. She was very desirous of establishing two churches beside Khergam. Bamanvel to the north was established in 1935, and permission was granted in 1945 to establish the other in the south at Wankal. This vision will surely come to fruition, we firmly believe.

Even at the age of seventy-one she had such interest in the Khergam and Bamanvel churches that in spite of great difficulties she would not spare herself but pressed on and returned to India. Here she visited these churches again and in her unique way encouraged them in their evangelistic work; but her physical difficulties increased and on February 16, 1946, she left this world and went home to the Father's house. She is no longer with us, but the Khergam and Bamanvel churches and the works she did in them will ever remain as memorials to her. The beautiful church at Khergam is named "Miss Shumaker Memorial Church." A great favorite with Miss Shumaker was Matthew 6:33. From 1927 until her death she kept this verse as a motto before the church and the community.

Truly, "unless a grain of wheat fall into the ground and die it abideth by itself alone; but if it die it bringeth forth much fruit." This is perfectly true of Miss Shumaker. Blessed be this great and devoted missionary!

· · ·

Ida C. Shumaker

Ruth B. Statler

She was sister to the brown skin;
   Loved and loving, she was kin
To all India. There her heart was,
   There her sympathies. What does
God require of those who love Him?
   All of heart and all of hand.
Willingly her all she gave Him
   In that lovely, sinful land.
India drank of her rich spirit,
   Sipped the goodness of her heart,
Then it claimed her mortal body;
   Now her ashes are a part
Of its brown soil, as her memory
   Lives in brown-skinned India's heart.

"Retreat," Miss Ida's Bulsar Home

Bulsar Church (rear) and Bible Lines

65

The Miss Sahebs in 1914

Front, left to right: Anna Eby, Olive Widdowson
Center: Eliza Miller, Ida Shumaker, B. Mary Royer
Back: Ida Himmelsbaugh, Sadie Miller, Kathryn Ziegler

66

Bulsar Missionaries About 1912

From left to right: Dr. A. Raymond Cottrell, J. M. Blough, Quincy A. Holsopple,
Ida Shumaker, Kathren Holsopple, Anna Blough, Dr. Laura Cottrell

Enjoying the Luscious Mango

The Wagoner family, Miss Ida and Aunty K.
Left to right: Jo Wagoner, Ellen Wagoner, J. E. Wagoner, Ida Shumaker,
Elizabeth Kintner and Beth Wagoner

67

Miss Ida at Wanki on Christmas Day, 1922

Ida Shumaker Visiting in a Vyara Village

The Jalalpor Bungalow

Miss Ida Loved the Children

The Banyan Vista on the Jalalpor Road

70

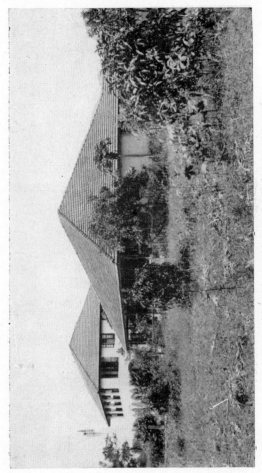

At Bulsar: Medical Bungalow and Number Two Bungalow

On the front veranda of the medical bungalow Miss Ida's funeral service was held

Missionaries Attending Mission Conference, 1937

Miss Ida is seen at the left-hand side of the front row

Fording the River Between Bulsar and Khergam

Miss Ida's First Home Near Khergam
She is in the tongo ready for a village trip

73

School Children and Village People at Khergam

A Khergam Schoolgirl

Khergam Congregation, 1930

75

Elder Naranji V. Solanki and Family

Naranji and Benabai
Co-workers with Ida Shumaker for many
years

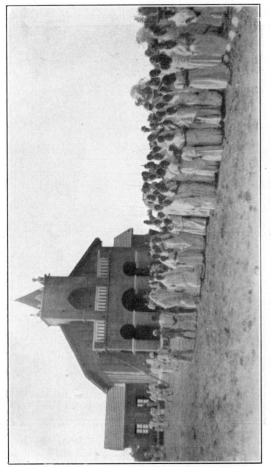

Dedication of Khergam Church, March 1934

Christian Workers in Bamanvel Village, Where
Khergam's Daughter Church Is Located

Aunt Ida, 1940
Margaret Brooks and Nina Alley are decorating Aunt Ida with flowers before she sails from India in 1940

Sister Ida
Among the dahlias in a friend's garden in Pennsylvania

English Cemetery at Bulsar

Miss Ida's final resting place, beside the graves of Mary Quinter, Rosa Kaylor, Andrew Butterbaugh, J. Elmer Wagoner, two Ebey children and three Bollinger children